Tsi-Min lives in China with her family and they have little to eat until Tsi-Min has a very special dream...

The Dream Child

A Bedtime Story

by Sylvia Marsh
illustrated by Gill Guile

Copyright © 1991 by World International Publishing Limited.
All rights reserved.
Published in Great Britain by World International Publishing Limited,
An Egmont Company, Egmont House, P.O.Box 111,
Great Ducie Street, Manchester M60 3BL.
Printed in DDR. ISBN 0 7498 0067 4

A CIP catalogue record for this book is available from the British Library

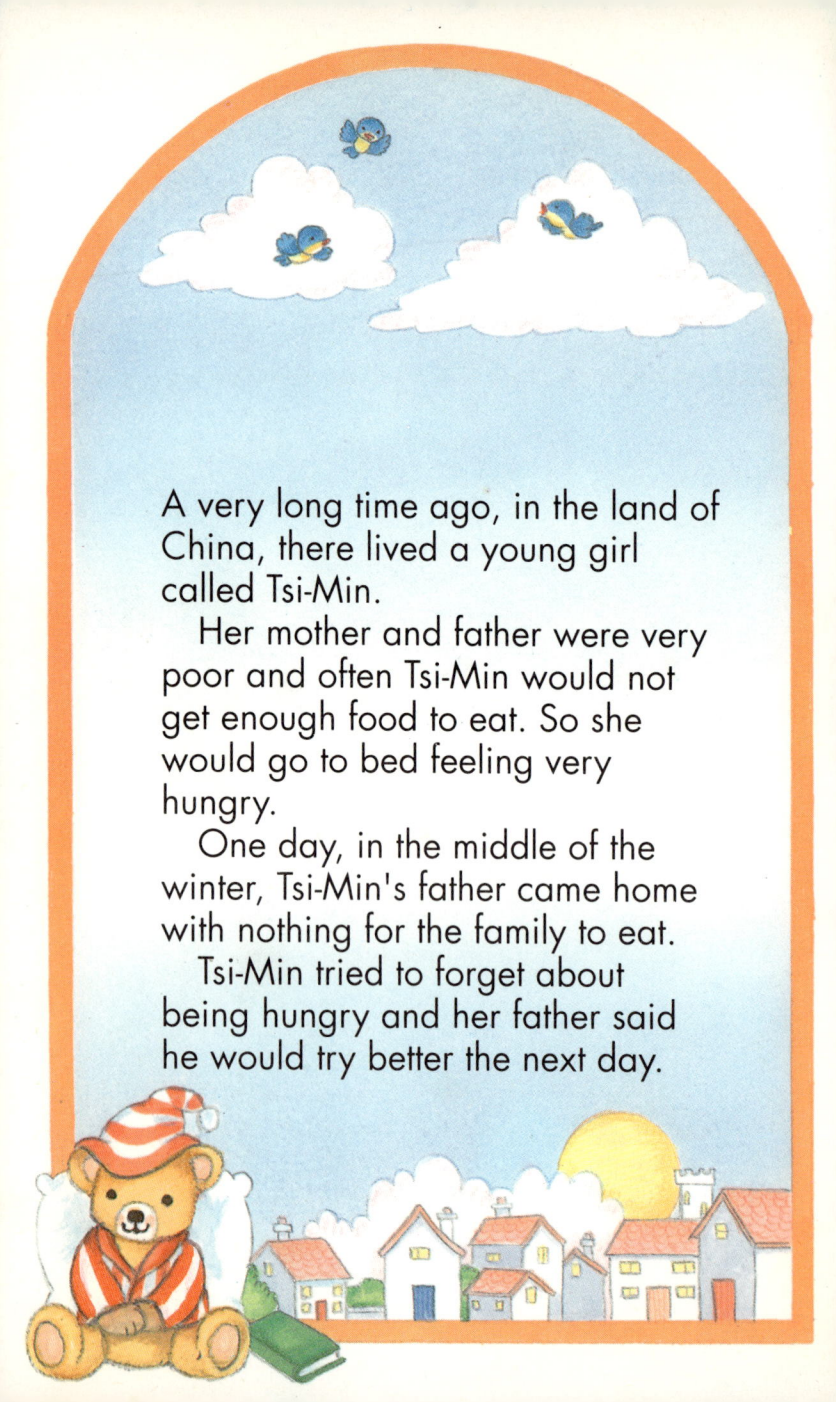

A very long time ago, in the land of China, there lived a young girl called Tsi-Min.

Her mother and father were very poor and often Tsi-Min would not get enough food to eat. So she would go to bed feeling very hungry.

One day, in the middle of the winter, Tsi-Min's father came home with nothing for the family to eat.

Tsi-Min tried to forget about being hungry and her father said he would try better the next day.

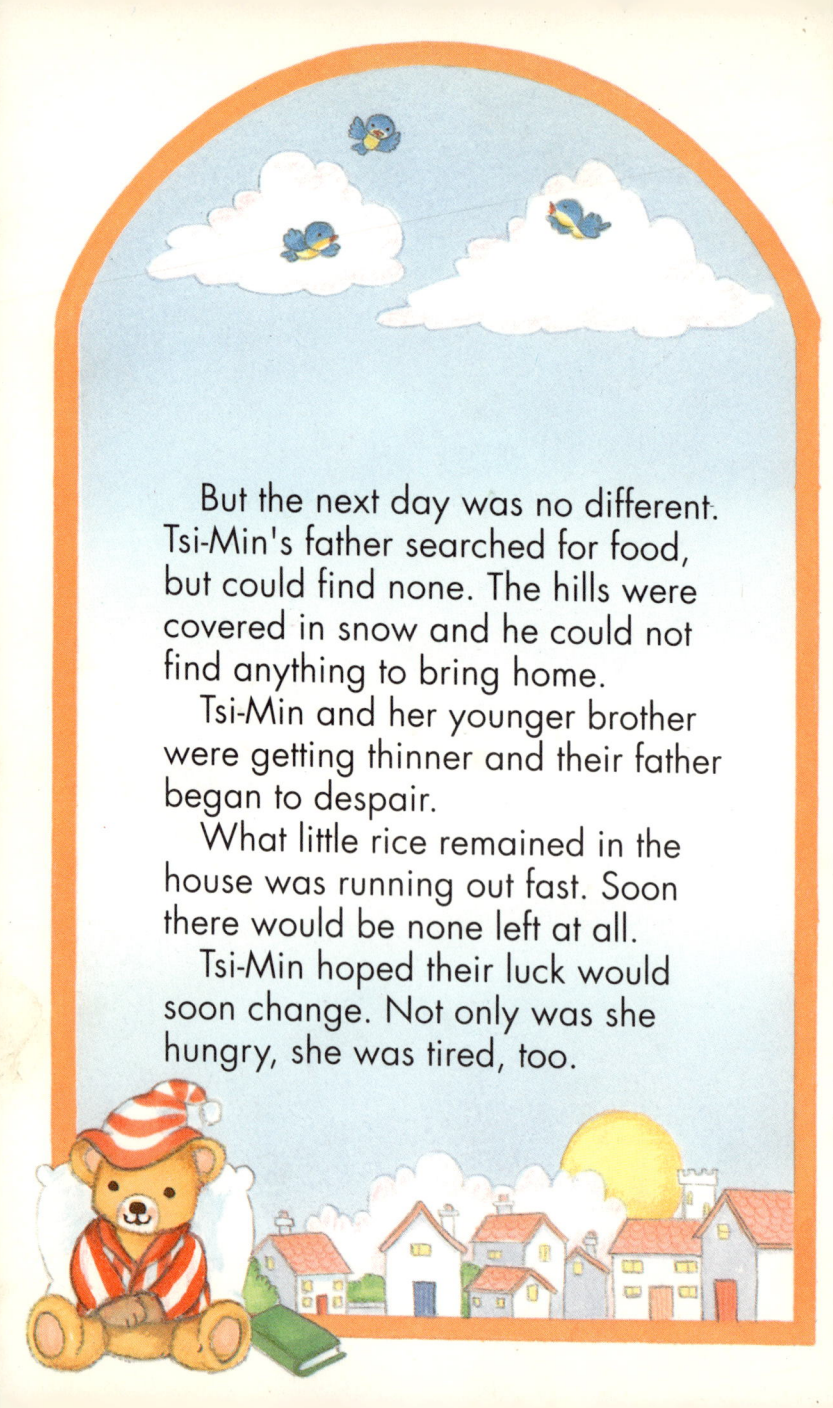

But the next day was no different. Tsi-Min's father searched for food, but could find none. The hills were covered in snow and he could not find anything to bring home.

Tsi-Min and her younger brother were getting thinner and their father began to despair.

What little rice remained in the house was running out fast. Soon there would be none left at all.

Tsi-Min hoped their luck would soon change. Not only was she hungry, she was tired, too.

That night, when Tsi-Min was fast asleep, she had a beautiful dream.

She dreamt she was dressed in silk clothes, in a great palace. She was standing at a wide table which was laden with delicious food of every kind imaginable. Tsi-Min could not believe her eyes.

But no sooner had she stretched out her hand to touch the lovely food than the dream faded away.

Tsi-Min awoke and looked around. There was no food to be seen. It had only been a dream.

In the morning Tsi-Min told her family about the dream.

They listened and wished that the dream might come true.

Tsi-Min told them so much about the food she had seen in her dream, that they began to imagine it was on the table before them.

But it had only been a dream and Tsi-Min's father knew he must go out once more to look for food.

All that day, Tsi-Min described the dream over and over again to her little brother.

That night Tsi-Min had another dream about the lovely palace.

Once more she dreamt she was wearing beautiful clothes, standing in front of a table laden with food.

Again she reached out to touch the food. But this time it did not vanish before her eyes.

Instead, she ate and ate until she could eat no more. Yet still the table was piled with food!

At last Tsi-Min stopped eating. Then she looked up and saw a strange little figure watching her.

It was a mandarin, dressed in the finest robes fit only for an emperor.

Tsi-Min bowed.

"Do not be afraid, Tsi-Min," said the mandarin. "I know all about your hunger. Eat as much food as you like."

Tsi-Min thanked the mandarin and said, "But, please, tell me how I came here. Surely I am in a dream?"

"Indeed you are, Tsi-Min," replied the mandarin. "This is the Palace of Dreams."

Tsi-Min thought for a while. "My family are hungry, too. Please may I take them some food from your wonderful table?"

The mandarin was silent, and he shook his head. "That cannot be, Tsi-Min," he said. "For this dream is for you alone."

Tsi-Min felt sad.

The mandarin could see this and he held out his hand towards her.

"Take this gift," he said, gently. "It is for you and your family. You shall go without food no more."

Slowly Tsi-Min's dream faded away, and she began to wake up.

In her hand she found a spoon.

At first she could not think how it had come to be there.

"I did not go to sleep with this spoon in my hand last night," she explained to her little brother.

"Then it must have been put there by someone," he said.

Tsi-Min thought hard. "Yes...it was!" said Tsi-Min, feeling excited as she began to remember her dream.

"Who?" asked Tsi-Min's brother.
"It was the mandarin!" she said. "I had another dream about the palace and this time I was allowed to eat the food on the table!"

Tsi-Min's brother could hardly believe his ears as his sister told him all about the delicious food.

"And then the mandarin gave me this spoon," she continued. "He said that none of us would go hungry ever again."

But how could an ordinary spoon help them?

Tsi-Min and her little brother wondered about the spoon all day.

When Tsi-Min's father came home that evening, once more he was empty-handed.

Now there were only a few grains of rice left in the house – not nearly enough to provide food for the family.

"How are we going to manage?" asked Tsi-Min's brother.

"Remember what the mandarin told me," she said, and they both looked at the spoon.

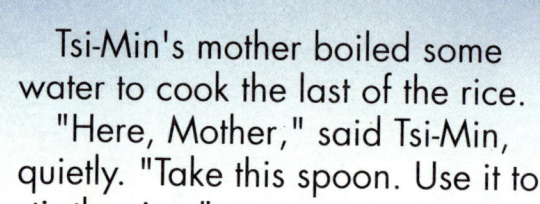

Tsi-Min's mother boiled some water to cook the last of the rice.

"Here, Mother," said Tsi-Min, quietly. "Take this spoon. Use it to stir the rice."

Tsi-Min gave the spoon to her mother.

Never could she have imagined what a wonderful thing was about to happen.

As her mother stirred the rice, the few grains seemed to multiply.

More and more appeared in the pan until it overflowed with rice!

"The mandarin was right — we shall not go without food after all!" cried Tsi-Min.

She took the spoon and stirred a jug of water. The water turned to wine! The family was overjoyed!

The news spread far and wide. People from all over China came to meet Tsi-Min. They listened as she told them of her dream.

From that day forth Tsi-Min was known throughout China by a new name: Tsi-Min Tu-Wan-San, which means 'The Child of the Dream'.

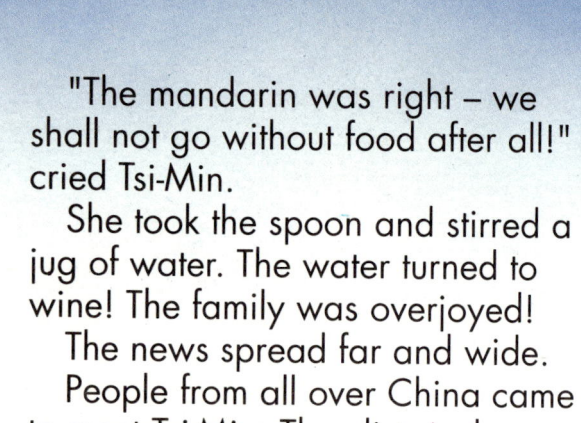